Explaining Darfur

Explaining Darfur

Four Lectures on the Ongoing Genocide by

Agnes van Ardenne-van der Hoeven
Mohamed Salih
Nick Grono
Juan Méndez

With an introduction by
Fouad Ibrahim

Vossiuspers UvA is an imprint of Amsterdam University Press.
This edition is established under the auspices of the University of Amsterdam.

Center for Holocaust and Genocide Studies
(University of Amsterdam, Royal Netherlands Academy of Arts and Sciences)

All photos: Michel de Groot
Cover design: René Staelenberg, Amsterdam
Lay-out: JAPES, Amsterdam

ISBN 978 90 5629 425 0
NUR 740

© Vossiuspers UvA, Amsterdam, 2006

Table of Contents

FOREWORD

"Call it civil war; call it ethnic cleansing; call it genocide; call it "none of the above." The reality is the same. There are people in Darfur who desperately need the help of the international community. "
Colin Powell's testimonial before the Senate Foreign Relations Committee
September 2004

The Center for Holocaust and Genocide Studies has been monitoring Darfur since the early signs and warnings of massive scale atrocities, which might have been contributing to genocide. As the Center is predominantly an institute for education and for creating knowledge and awareness about large-scale crimes against humanity, Darfur has been high on its agenda for a number of years.

Some smaller events on the situation in Darfur were organised 2004, but, while the developments in the Darfur-area deteriorated and public media attention decreased, we felt the need to organize a substantial event, which would increase awareness and provide a thorough and deeper knowledge of the human catastrophe in Darfur. That is how together with involved students from Humanity in Action, an international human rights network, the idea of this lecture cycle originated. Our intent was to invite experts from various backgrounds with different perspectives on this pressing issue. The goal of the lecture cycle was to pass on knowledge to a larger audience on the ongoing crimes against humanity committed in Sudan, Darfur. The wide range of areas we tried to encompass are reflected in the topics and respectively the choice of speakers: the Dutch policy, the academic analysis, NGO insights and the international political perspective.

Our deepest gratitude goes out to the lecturers: Minister of Development Cooperation, Agnes Van Ardenne-Van der Hoeve, professor Mohammed Salih, professor Fouad Ibrahim, Nick Grono of the International Crisis Group, Leslie Lefkow of Human Rights Watch and Juan Mendez, UN Special Adviser to the Secretary General on the Prevention of Genocide. They have been willing and able to find the time and made the effort to come to Amsterdam for their inspiring lectures and commentaries.

With this publication of the lecture cycle, we hope to reach a greater public audience and provide background information on the mass atrocities in Darfur. We hope that this will contribute to a better understanding of the complicated conflict and, in some way, add to a solution in the near future. The Center for Holocaust and Genocide Studies will continue to monitor and research the situation, in order to prevent Darfur from being forgotten now and remembered later as a humanitarian disaster that could have been prevented. In the end, we hope that violence will be halted, justice restored and peace will prevail.

In conclusion, we hope that our readers do not entirely view this publication as a matter of shared information, but also as a matter of shared responsibility.

On behalf of the Center for Holocaust and Genocide Studies and Humanity in Action,

Silvia Rottenberg   Jacqueline Bouscher
Vica Bogaerts   Ykje Vriesinga

Fouad Ibrahim

INTRODUCTION TO THE CONFLICT IN DARFUR/WEST SUDAN

The following introduction is meant to provide the reader with some background information that might be useful for a better understanding of the guest authors' contributions in this volume. We will highlight the central issues and explain the roles of the main actors in the ongoing war in Darfur before referring to the different positions of the contributors to this volume.

Speaking of a "conflict" in Darfur means, in fact, playing down a horrible genocide as confirmed by the US Congress and various human rights organizations. However, the UN Commission of Inquiry has not been able to discover hard facts proving that the Sudan Government has intentionally pursued a policy of genocide. Yet, it concluded that this government is responsible for serious violations of internationally recognized human rights, including rights under international law. Thus, while legal experts are indulging themselves in hair-splitting debates on the definition of genocide, the Commission admits that the Sudan Government and its proxy militias continue conducting "indiscriminate attacks, including killing civilians, torture, enforced disappearances, destruction of villages, rape and other forms of sexual violence, pillaging and forced displacement, throughout Darfur" (UN Commission of Inquiry, as cited in this volume by Grono, p. 41).

The failure of the UN legal experts to prove genocide in Darfur appears to have been welcomed by governments throughout the world, for it freed them of the commitment to immediately stop the killings of civilians in Darfur, as is stipulated in the UN Convention on the Prevention and Punishment of the Crime of Genocide of 1948. Instead of taking action, the international community is trying to clear its conscience by offering humanitarian aid and financing the expenses of the African Union Mission in Sudan (AMIS), the peace talks in Abuja and the prosecutions made by the International Criminal Court (ICC) in The Hague. Thus, the Darfur genocide is reduced to a "low intensity conflict", threatened by complete oblivion.

The setting of the conflict: Darfur and its population (cf. Fig. 1)

Darfur lies in the farthest west of the Republic of the Sudan, bordering Chad and Central Africa. It covers an area of about 508,000 km², which is almost equal to the area covered by the Netherlands, Germany, Austria and Switzerland together. Due to its great north-south extension of about 1,140 km, Darfur is transversed by several climatic-vegetational zones, ranging from the hot, hyper-arid desert in the north to the woodland savannah with 900 mm of mean annual precipitation in the south. The thornscrub savannah of central Darfur is interrupted by the wetter region of the Jebel Marra massif (3,088 m), which receives 500-1000 mm of mean annual rainfall.

The Jebel Marra massif and its forelands are the main settlement areas of the Fur sedentary people, after whom the region is called "Darfur", i.e. "homeland of the Fur". Located within the Sahelian zone, it was struck by several drought disasters during the last three decades. The occurring famines would have been less severe, had it not been for the systematic marginalization of Darfur by the successive governments since the British conquered the once autonomous sultanate and annexed it to their Sudanese colony in 1916. For centuries, independent Darfur has been able to sustain its population and cope with the drought crises, which are part and parcel of the region due to its climatic pattern. Even today, despite the long-time neglect and marginalization by the Khartoum Government, the seven million Darfuris would be able to sustain themselves if only they could live in peace.

There exists a widespread fallacy, which is created and propagated by the Khartoum Government and adopted by western journalists and politicians, that the main reason behind the violence occurring in Darfur is the competition over scarce water resources and pastures, which were degraded by drought in recent times and became desertified. Admittedly, squabbles between nomads and the settled population occasionally occurred when nomadic herds intruded into and destroyed the fields of the small-scale farmers. However, such conflicts were usually resolved according to the traditional tribal laws, and they seldom resulted in tribal wars of a larger scale. By adopting the Sudan Government's definition of the presently occurring crimes against humanity as competition over natural resources, western politicians are once again trying to quiet their consciences and to free themselves of the obligation

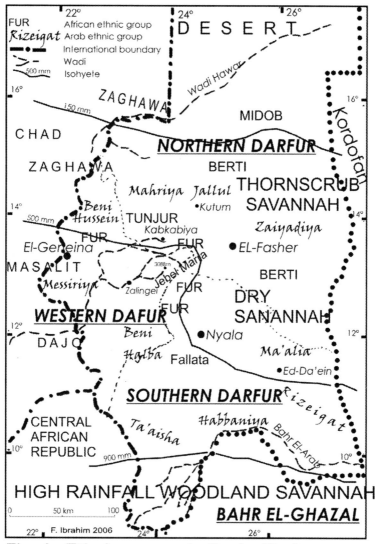

Fig. 1   Ethnic groups in Darfur/Sudan

for international commitment to stop them, including using military intervention as a last resort.

In Darfur, there live about eighty ethnic groups. Following the current discourse, we should differentiate between the groups which define themselves as "Arabs" and those which define themselves according to their respective indigenous groups. The latter are collectively called *zurga*, i.e. "blacks" by the "Arabs". Some of these African ethnic groups, such as the Berti and the Tunjur, lost their indigenous languages long ago. Today, most African groups in Darfur speak Sudanese-Darfuri Arabic as a lingua franca, in addition to their respective African languages. The "Arabs" call these languages *rutana* (an onomatopoetic expression meaning "incomprehensible, nonsensical articulations"). The Arab Muslims of the Nile valley, especially the Dja'liyin, have succeeded in spreading the ideology that being an Arab and speaking Arabic correctly is an essential prerequisite for being a proper Muslim. This, in addition to the heritage of the conflict as being one between slave-hunters and those who were forced into slavery, led to the creation of an inferiority complex among some of the African ethnic groups. It makes them exert great efforts to this day to teach their children good Arabic and urge them to learn as much as possible of the Qur'an by heart. Some Africans even try to prove their Arab descent, or possibly an ancestry related to the prophet himself, by written pedigrees (El-Tom 2004). The largest African group are the Fur, to whom approximately one million persons belong. Other major African groups are the Zaghawa in the northwest and the Masalit in the west of Darfur, each of them numbering about 350,000 persons. The Zaghawa of Darfur are related to the Zaghawa living in Chad. The fact that Idriss Deby, the present Chadian president is a member of this ethnic group, has linked the Darfur conflict to the more recent insurgence in eastern Chad, thus rendering it international.

The groups which define themselves as Arabs were until recently nomadic pastoralists, but of late became semi-nomads, settled smallholders or town dwellers. However, they still stick to their old identities either as *Baggara* (cattle herders) or *Abbala* (camel herders). Despite their relatively small numbers, the *Abbala* and the *Baggara* Arabs command a larger territory than the more numerous settled African populations. Being less mobile, the latter had to confine themselves to the limited areas with permanent traditional water sources.

In the 1990s, pursuing its policy of "divide and rule", the Central Government divided Darfur into three *wilayat* (states): Northern Darfur, Southern Darfur and Western Darfur, with their respective capitals El-Fasher, Nyala and El-Geneina. The inhabitants of these towns are ethnically heterogeneous. At the top of the social pyramid in these towns we find the influential Arabs of the Nile valley as well as the rich Arabs of Darfur. The majority of the town dwellers forming the basis of the social pyramid are poor, drought-stricken or civil-war-stricken displaced persons, mostly Africans of rural origin. The thin middle-class includes low-paid civil servants, small traders and artisans of mixed origins.

The warring parties

Besides the myth of the scarce economic resources as a root cause of the war in Darfur, another misconception created by the Sudan Government is that the so-called Darfuri "rebels" were the ones who had begun the war. Yet, the Government armed the Arab militias (Janjaweed) as early as the mid-1980s, and the present Government formed by the National Islamic Front (NIF) incorporated the Janjaweed into the paramilitary Popular Defence Forces (PDF) in the 1990s. The Arab militias had originally been targeted at the Dinka African ethnic group of Bahr El-Ghazal (South West Sudan) and were responsible for the notorious "Massacre of Ed-Da'ein" of 1987, in which thousands of helpless Dinka were burnt alive in cargo-train wagons or killed in displaced settlements. When in preparation for the Comprehensive Peace Accord of January 2005 the Government ordered the Arab militias to stop their raids against the southern Sudanese, the Janjaweed shifted their activities northwards and started attacking the Masalit, the Fur and the Zaghawa, thus pursuing their own agenda of gaining more land and power in Darfur. The Government supported the Janjaweed because political opposition had been gaining ground among the indigenous African population. After the Janjaweed had already killed no less than 2,000 Africans, some fractions of the Fur and the Zaghawa made an armed insurgence against the Central Government and its proxy militias in February 2003. It started small, but soon gained impetus, when the atrocities of the Government troops and the Janjaweed caused a large number of desperate Africans to join the insurgence. The conflict escalated when the Government air forces bombarded hundreds of villages and its troops joined the Janjaweed in a large-scale scorched-earth war against the helpless civilians.

In the mean time, the US and the EU were finalising the Comprehensive Peace Accord, to bring the 21-year-old civil war in southern Sudan to an end. Nobody was ready to jeopardize the peace prospects for the south by accusing the Sudan Government of opening up a new front for committing war crimes in Darfur. The EU alone had pledged 4.3 billion Euro of aid to the Sudan in connection with that peace accord. To stop the rich flow of funds because of the atrocities in Darfur would endanger the long-negotiated peace accord for the south. The Sudan Government, fully aware of this difficult situation of western diplomacy, uses it and disregards all international threats.

Options for a conflict solution

From the point of view of the fighting parties, war seems to be the only solution available. The insurgents, mainly the Sudan Liberation Movement/Army (SLM/SLA) and the Justice and Equality Movement (JEM), maintain that they have taken up arms as a last resort. For years, they had appealed to state president Al-Bashir to put an end to the marginalization of Darfur and to protect the indigenous Africans against the constant attacks of the Arab Janjaweed, whose obvious intention is to expand their territory and power at the cost of the African ethnic groups. Al-Bashir, in his turn, is determined to use all brutal means to crush the Darfur rebellion, for in case it succeeded, this would encourage the upheavals that started already in other parts of the country, such as in the Nuba Mountains, the Blue Nile Province and Eastern Sudan. He is aware of the fact that any equitable peace agreement in Darfur would entail a serious loss of power for his Government and its loyal Arab groups.

The authors who contributed to this volume do not believe that war is the only solution, but rather the worst one. Thus, they suggest various other ways of solving the problem. Agnes van Ardenne-van der Hoeven, Dutch Minister of Development Cooperation, and Mohamed Salih favour a democratization of the Sudan as a long-term solution. The Minister considers the Comprehensive Peace Accord of 2005 as a landmark in political reform and an indicator of the building of an equitable national government, which would also end the marginalization of Darfur and the other peripheral regions. Mohamed Salih's main concern is, on the other hand, the growing ethnical identification and exclusion of the political parties and the way this development is used by the ruling National Islamic Front (NIF). Salih explains how this tendency contradicts with the basics of good governance. Many had cherished hopes that the non-Muslim leaders of southern Sudan would support the Darfur cause. But they are at the moment strongly indulged in their own internal hostilities.

According to Nick Grono, the best option to try and end the situation in Darfur is by expanding the manpower, tasks and technical equipment of the African Union troops. He would like them to have a larger mandate and factual capability in controlling the militias and protecting the civilians. In January 2006, the UN Secretary General went even further and suggested that the US and the EU send troops under UN command, as it had become clear that the AMIS had failed to restore security in Darfur. In my belief, the international community is spending billions of US dollars on a futile attempt to restore security and stop killings of civilians in Darfur, while one brief order from Sudan's president Al-Bashir could make the Janjaweed put an end to their attacks, as happened in the wake of the signing of the Comprehensive Peace Accord, when raids against the Dinka of Bahr El-Ghazal stopped as soon as the order from Khartoum came.

Juan E. Mendez is suggesting a fairly comprehensive plan of action for the Darfur problem. One item of this plan is discussed here for its paramount importance. It concerns the involvement of the grassroots people in the peacemaking process, which means intertribal negotiations at the local level. In fact, the Arabs and the Africans who are currently fighting each other, coexisted and intensively interacted with each other to their mutual advantage for many centuries. In the course of time, they developed traditional institutions for conflict solution, which are still functioning today. The central part of these institutions is the tribal reconciliation conference (*mu'tamar as-sulh al-qabali*). Recognizing this, the Sudan Government organized such a conference in Khartoum in August 2004. However, peace could not be brought to Darfur through this as the hosting party lacked impartiality. New tribal reconciliation conferences could nevertheless prove to again be a fruitful method. Because of the large dimension of the conflict, the conferences should be held not once, but more frequently, and in all the various administrative districts of the region.

The aim of such traditional conferences is to restore peace by reconciling the fighting parties. Unlike the western judicial systems, peace is not attained by punishing the wrongdoers, but by compensating the victims or their families. The culprits' tribe as a whole bears the responsibility of paying the compensations once these have been agreed on. According to the traditional law, *diya*, i.e. "blood money", is paid, sometimes in the form of cattle, for those who were killed. The fact that the conflicting parties in Darfur are all Muslims enhances the chances of success of such conferences, to which religious leaders, mostly from the pacifist Sufi brotherhoods, are usually invited as mediators. Western politicians may think that the Darfur disaster is too great a cause to be adequately resolved by methods of conflict resolution, which they consider obsolete. But one should be reminded of what happened in Iraq in August 2004, when an old and physically weak man, the Great Ayatollah Ali el-Sistani, succeeded within hours in putting an end to a similarly brutal conflict, which the Americans and their allies had failed to resolve in months.

However, the Darfur insurgents rightly fear that such traditional conferences would hardly address the fundamental structural issues pertaining to the decades-long marginalization of the African ethnic groups of Darfur. But one should agree with Mendez that local intercommunal reconciliation is a necessity and must precede all other steps if one wants to reach peace in Darfur. Tribal reconciliation conferences in the Sudan guarantee that the culprits acknowledge their wrong doings and compensate for the damage caused by them against the lives and the property of others. We must also remember that in Islamic as well as in African traditional law, compensation and reconciliation are the fundamental prerequisites of peace making.

It goes without saying that other measures have to be undertaken simultaneously to reach a sustainable peace in Darfur. So, the international community should strongly support the Abuja talks between the Sudan Government and the main insurgent groups to help them reach a peace agreement, which could be a foundation for equity and good governance in Darfur (cf. Mohamed Salih's contribution). And since the negotiation of a lasting peace in Darfur unfortunately could take months, if not years, humanitarian assistance from the part of the international community should be intensified, even if the Sudan Government tries to prevent it, in order to reduce the high mortality rate among the two million displaced persons, especially innocent women and children.

References

Anonymous: *The Black Book – Imbalance of Power and Wealth in Sudan.* Part 1 (in Arabic): Khartoum 2000. Part 2 (2003; in Arabic): http://www. sudanjem.com Parts 1 and 2 (2004; English translation): http://www.sudanjem.com

El-Tom, A.O. (2004): *Darfur People: Too Black for the Arab-Islamic Project of Sudan.* http://www.sudanjem.com

Ibrahim, F.N. (1984): *Ecological Imbalance in the Republic of the Sudan – with Reference to Desertification in Darfur.* Bayreuth.

Ibrahim, F.N. (1988): *Conflict Solution Among the Hadandawa – Transition from the Madlas to the Court of Law.* In: Ibrahim, F.N.; Ruppert, H. (eds.): *Rural-Urban Migration and Identity Change. Case Studies from the Sudan.* Bayreuther Geowissenschaftliche Arbeiten, vol. 11, Bayreuth. pp.157-168.

Ibrahim, F. (2004a): *Völkermord in Darfur – Verbrannte Erde.* Pogrom – bedrohte Völker, H. 6. Göttingen. pp. 16-19.

Ibrahim, F. (2004b): *Darfur – Hintergründe eines Konflikts.* In: Die Tageszeitung (TAZ), 9.8.04. Berlin. p. 4.

United Nations (January 2005): *Report of the International Commission of the Inquiry on Darfur to the United Nations Secretary General.* http:// www.un.org/News/dh/sudan/com_inq_darfur.pdf

Agnes van Ardenne-van der Hoeven

THE ROAD TO DARFUR LEADS THROUGH KHARTOUM

1 November 2005

Life is hard on the plains of Darfur. It was hard enough for Kaltuma Hasala Adan and her family to scrape out a living on the edge of the desert, even before the sky came crashing down. In January 2004, her village was bombed. While Kaltuma was still mourning for her 18-month-old baby, who was killed in the attack, Arab horsemen came to finish the job. After they had killed her 15-year-old son, Issa, they threw his body into the well to contaminate the water. That same day, Kaltuma's husband disappeared. Four months and many attacks later, she finally left her crops and livestock behind and took her three surviving children to a refugee camp across the border in Chad. Thousands of her fellow Darfurians were already there. Terrorised and terrified.

Stories like Kaltuma's break our hearts. Now that we live in a global village, we can no longer plead ignorance when villages are burned to the ground. Images of desperate women like Kaltuma reach our own safe, comfortable living rooms on television or the Internet. We can never say that we did not know. And looking back, we must not say that we did not act. We have a responsibility to protect the unprotected. No civilised person wants to stand aside as wells are contaminated with the bodies of slaughtered children. Some of you might think that it would be best to just send in an army. This is understandable, given the atrocities we have seen in Darfur. But the main question we have to ask ourselves before taking action is: how can we effectively resolve the crisis and help the victims, without escalating the situation or planting the seeds of new conflict? As I will argue, in this context, sending in the troops would be both unwise and impossible. At this stage, the only viable option is a policy that integrates political pressure, diplomacy, active peacekeeping and humanitarian assistance. I will also argue that the international community urgently needs to step up its efforts in these areas, not just in Darfur but especially in the peace process between the north and south of Sudan. The key to peace in Darfur is a stable and democratic government of national unity in Khartoum. But in order to fully understand the complexity of the situation on the ground, we should first explore the origins of the violence in Darfur.

The conflict

"Night comes to the desert all at once, as if someone turned off the light." These words, written by the American novelist Joyce Carol Oates, have taken on a sinister meaning for the people of Darfur. For centuries, African subsistence farmers and Arab nomadic herders, all of them Muslims, coexisted there on the edge of the Sahara Desert. In fact, they did more than coexist – they also cooperated. For example, after the farmers had harvested a crop, the nomads would bring their cattle and camels to eat the residue and fertilise the soil. This symbiosis ensured the survival of both groups.

But in time, this delicate balance was disturbed as a population boom coincided with environmental collapse. Over the past century, the population of Darfur increased by 500 per cent and the number of sheep by 900 per cent. At the same time, climate change, overgrazing and uncontrolled logging have destroyed the ecosystem. Every year, the desert advances another five kilometres to the south. And as the desert gains ground, conflict, rather than cooperation, has become the main survival strategy. In the past, conflicts over land were resolved through traditional law and negotiation. But in the eighties and nineties, with central government turning a blind eye, the people of Darfur began to beat their ploughshares into swords. Cultural identities became politicised and there were outbreaks of violence. At the turn of the millennium, the conflict escalated as the two main rebel forces began to attack the central government. Night fell, as if someone had turned off the light.

It was Darfur's darkest hour. For many years, the farmers there had felt that the central government in Khartoum was discriminating against them. The two main rebel groups, the Sudan Liberation Movement and the Justice and Equality Movement, seized control of an airport in protest and destroyed some government aeroplanes and helicopters. The government responded to the rebel attacks with brute force. It armed the Arab Janjaweed militia and unleashed it on the civilian population of Darfur. On people like Kaltuma and her family. Tens of thousands died. Two million were displaced. With human rights violations ranging from political imprisonment and torture to rape and amputation.

This eruption of violence set off a worldwide debate about whether genocide was taking place. In September 2004, six months after Kaltuma's family and her village were destroyed, Colin Powell and the US congress answered this question in the affirmative. But, in January of this year, an international commission concluded that there was no evidence that the Sudanese government had ever adopted or implemented a policy of genocide in Darfur.

Should we send in the troops?

Obviously, the lack of evidence of genocide does not mean that the international community should remain passive. The international commission of inquiry did uncover extremely serious violations of human rights and humanitarian law. As you all know, the Security Council has therefore decided to refer Darfur to the ICC. Again, we have an obligation to protect the unprotected – whoever they are and wherever they live. During the recent UN summit, 191 world leaders confirmed this when they embraced the principle of a responsibility to protect. This is not a responsibility to roll out the tanks whenever human rights are trampled with impunity. Instead, it is the responsibility of the international community to make use of the full range of foreign policy instruments, including humanitarian aid, diplomacy and peacekeeping. Each conflict is different and requires a different mix of responses.

Military intervention will prove to be an appropriate and practical solution only in some cases. In others, it would only make matters worse in the short run or plant the seeds of new conflicts in the long run. In Darfur today, military intervention would do more harm than good. Moreover, it would not be a feasible course of action. It is a political fact that there is insufficient support in the UN Security Council for such an intervention, and, in fact, it has never even been on the agenda. And only a Security Council resolution under Chapter VII of the UN Charter could endow a military operation with international legitimacy. But even in the unlikely case that the Security Council suddenly adopted such a resolution – even then, Darfur's terrain and its poor infrastructure would make for an extremely risky and dangerous mission. And firm resolutions by the UN do not always translate into firm action by UN member states. Few governments would be willing or able to obtain enough public and parliamentary support to deploy troops.

I believe that it is not only impossible to send in the troops, for political and practical reasons, but also undesirable at this time. It would jeopardise the only long-term solution to the grievances of the people of Darfur: political dialogue. Pulling a gun would, without a doubt, make it impossible to conduct any type of diplomacy in the foreseeable future. Darfur's problems began when a situation of peaceful coexistence on the edge of the desert collapsed because of population pressure and environmental degradation. Only at the negotiating table can the feuding parties restore the balance between ethnic groups and between mankind and nature.

Glimmers of hope

This leaves the international community with the formidable task of ensuring the success of these vital negotiations and providing critical humanitarian assistance. We can take encouragement from a recent diplomatic milestone. In January 2005, the Comprehensive Peace Agreement put an end to the longest war in the history of the modern world: the conflict between the north and south of Sudan, in which some two million people were killed and four million displaced. The Netherlands played a crucial part in brokering the peace deal. Two years ago in Noordwijk, I organised the first meeting between the two main parties to the conflict, the Government of Sudan and the Sudan People's Liberation Army. And we also put our money where our mouth is: we already made 200 million euros available for the reconstruction phase. A phase, which should start right away, as far as we are concerned.

The peace agreement between the north and the south, which led to a Government of National Unity last September, has built momentum for the peace talks on Darfur. This government is possibly better placed than the previous one when it comes to resolving the Darfur conflict. I was one of the first to drive home this message to the government in Khartoum. Along with the north-south peace accord and the start of the Darfur peace talks, the African Union has offered another glimmer of hope. African leaders have declared that they wanted to take responsibility for their continent and deal with its conflicts themselves. Of course, this is in their own interest: when the biggest country in Africa is in flames, the fire also threatens other countries in the region. The Security Council has welcomed the African initiative and authorised the African Union to deploy a monitoring mission in Darfur.

The faltering response of the international community

Apart from these glimmers of hope, I am sad to say that the international community is not rising to the occasion in Sudan. It's all too little, too late. Now that the world's attention is focused on Iraq, the scandals in the UN and the earthquake in Kashmir, we seem to be forgetting about Sudan. Obviously, the primary responsibility for solving Sudan's problems lies with the Sudanese government and people. But we have seen that international involvement can mean the difference between war and peace. So where is the international community's sense of urgency, about both Darfur and the north-south peace process? Isn't it clear that peace in Darfur is dependent on the successful implementation of the peace agreement in the north and the south? The road to Darfur leads through Khartoum.

We still see Darfur as an isolated crisis. But Darfur is a piece of the Sudan puzzle. Only when the country is at peace and on its way to prosperity will we be able to address the underlying causes of the problems in the Darfur region. The key to getting the entire country back on track is the successful implementation of the peace accord between north and south. By focusing solely on Darfur, we are missing the bigger picture. Again, I am sad to say, this message has not gotten through to the international community. The UN Mission in the south, UNMIS, is still not fully deployed. The international community's failure to follow through translates directly into insecurity on the ground. For example, yesterday, two deminers were killed by Ugandan rebels of the LRA who are apparently still at large in the south of Sudan. We must also get reconstruction off the ground. The south needs roads, schools and hospitals. If we don't help the people who are trying to rebuild their country, hope might lose out to hatred, and cooperation to conflict. Unless we invest in peace now, the Sudanese people will see no peace dividend. Unfortunately, things are not moving fast enough at a time when many refugees from the south are returning home. They need to see progress. They need our help.

But the UN does not see the need to set up camps for refugees returning to the south of Sudan. A massive influx of refugees has been taking place, but, apparently, UN officials have had their backs turned. With little help in sight, those refugees are now leaving rural areas behind to try their luck in the cities, which already have more than enough problems. The Netherlands has offered 20 million euros to the UN for activities that will yield rapid results on the ground. This offer was probably lying around on a UN official's desk for months, because it took a very long time before the UN could come up with proposals for spending the money. The Sudan test comes at a crucial time for the United Nations, just after the summit where world leaders tried to re-establish trust. But the UN organisations have to earn that trust every day. Not in the conference room, but out there in Sudan. And I believe that to deliver the goods there, the UN needs to cooperate more efficiently and to avoid overlap.

But other organisations are also failing to respond adequately, not just in Darfur, but in the country as a whole. The EU urgently needs to show the world its relevance and effectiveness. But like the UN, it is not rising to the challenge. So far, the EU has been disappointingly slow in putting money on the table and reluctant to send experts to the field. It has also failed to put enough political pressure on the African Union to make planning and logistics more efficient.

Unlike the UN and the EU, the African Union is still a young organisation, learning how to manage a monitoring mission by trial and error. But the Africans are so determined to solve this crisis themselves that they are reluctant to accept planning and logistics help from the outside. While the AU does accept money, it does not like to see Western faces in its headquarters. When the Netherlands supplied critical communications equipment, the AU left it in a repository for two months before putting it to use. The people of Darfur have no time for this.

The Netherlands' Darfur policy

As the nations of Africa take control of their own destiny, the Netherlands stands beside them. Our integrated Darfur policy, aimed at promoting lasting peace and sustainable development, has four components. First, political pressure. Over the past few years, I have personally visited Sudan five times. Every time, I brought up the issue of Darfur with officials at the highest levels of the Sudanese government. Our diplomacy also aims to constructively engage neighbouring countries in the process, such as Libya and Chad, who have so far been less than helpful. Libya should refrain from parallel peace brokering, while Chad should stop propping up rebel factions in Darfur. In March of this year, I went to Darfur myself, where I witnessed at first hand its heartbreaking misery and deep-rooted problems. I felt powerless and frustrated, of course. But the experience also strengthened my conviction that we must find a long-term solution for the people of Darfur through effective diplomacy. So that Kaltuma and her three surviving children can return home and build a new life, beyond the shadow of violence and poverty.

The Netherlands is also playing an important role in the Abuja peace talks, both through financial contributions and through the mediation of our ambassador-at-large, Wim Wessels. This is the second element of our policy. While the atmosphere has generally been good, the pace of progress has been very slow. The recent resurgence of violence in Darfur shows that not all factions feel they are represented in Abuja. That is why we are doing everything we can to make sure that everybody's interests are taken into account at the negotiating table. We are also doing everything we can to promote a swift agreement. The year 2005 opened with a peace accord between the north and the south – let us see to it that it ends with another one in the west.

The third component of our approach to Darfur is our financial and logistic support for the African Union mission. For example, the Netherlands has provided crucial expertise, sending two military observers, a police expert, an intelligence officer and an operations planner. But, as I said before, AMIS could be more effective if the Africans would swallow their pride and accept more international assistance. This is all the more important given the recent upsurge of violence, which is endangering both aid workers and the people they are trying to help.

The fourth and final priority of our Darfur policy is humanitarian assistance. While the politicians and diplomats talk inside the conference room and while AMIS is building strength to restore security, we must never forget the basic needs of the people. Dutch aid provides them with food, health care, water and sanitation. This year, a total contribution of almost 50 million euros has made Sudan the single biggest recipient of Dutch humanitarian assistance. And that aid has been effective: for example, mortality rates have fallen below UN standards for a humanitarian crisis.

Conclusion

Let me conclude. Kaltuma's children should not grow up in a refugee camp in Chad, relying on charity for food and security. The international community must rise to the occasion and, in particular, give the implementation of the peace agreement in the north and the south a big push in the right direction. If that accord is successful, then peace will also have a chance in Darfur. This is the only way to turn swords into ploughshares again. And a successful democratic government uniting Muslims and Christians could serve as a model for Africa and nearby nations in the Middle East.

If we succeed in putting Sudan on the path to lasting peace and sustainable development, Kaltuma's children will have the opportunity to continue their traditional way of life, at peace with the other peoples of the region and with their environment. Then Kaltuma and her family can say, in the words of a traditional song, "Let peace prevail. Cleanse your conscience, keep prosperity alive. The Moura Hill now wears a green shawl. Take up your sickles, drop your weapons."

M. A. Mohamed Salih

AFRICA'S GOVERNANCE DEFICIT, GENOCIDE, AND
ETHNOCIDE

15 November 2005

This paper is set out to articulate the relationship between governance deficit and crimes against humanity, ethnocide and genocide. Although it draws much on Sudan's Darfur crisis, reference will be made to other cases of human rights violations in Africa to highlight the broader relevance of governance deficit in cases that could potentially lead to genocide. This possibility increases if the resounding early warnings of an impending genocide are not taken seriously.

I attempt to offer a commentary on major cases of governance deficit in Africa. These are alarming, as they may develop into acts of to genocide and ethnocide. Nevertheless, I argue that justice can prevail in countries with severe governance deficit, when crimes against humanity are brought to a sharp focus and are acted upon. This is firstly a task for the Africans themselves, and then, equally important, for the global governance regime.

Conditions for Good Governance

Governance generally entails that those who exercise political, economic, and administrative authority to manage their citizens' affairs should be held accountable to the governed through institutionalised legal and administrative instruments and regulatory frameworks. Although governance has acquired strong economic connotations in respect to the global economic governance institutions (World Bank and the IMF), it transcends economics to other spheres of human existence.[1] Broadly, governance refers to the way power is exercised in managing the social, legal, political and economic institutions that regulate citizen affairs. This includes the rule of law, respect for human rights, an independent and effective judiciary, maintenance of civil peace and order, ensuring citizens' voices, freedom of information, respect for civil, cultural, political and economic rights, financial and auditing processes and accounting standards that ensure transparency, accountability amongst others.

Good governance means "democratic governance", which denotes that for any government to be legitimate, its authority and, thus, the legitimate exercise of power should derive from periodic, regular, free and fair contested elections through an inclusive participatory process. The question then is whether a convergence of governance as a desirable condition and governance as a practice could be found and acted upon. It is safe to argue that the promotion of good governance has gathered pace and gradually seeps through almost all policy-making, implementation and evaluation endeavours.[2]

Although many argue that the general tenets of governance are prevalent only in mature western democracies or claim that the concept is western - both in content and practice- it should not lead to denial of positive universalistic values. Essentially, the problem is not the positive attributes of governance as much as it is the attempts to superimpose governance regimes for the sake of political expediency. In this vain, it is obvious that difficulties with governance may emerge when noble concepts such as "good governance" are misconstrued for a practice of its positive universalistic values, but remain devoid of context, messages and meanings peculiar to a particular society.

Generally, one could argue that African specific governance, such as local conflict management governance, would resonate the universalistic conception of "good governance" immersed in a local context. It could provide good mechanisms for achieving peace in war stricken countries or in situations such as that of Darfur.

In reality, not all local governance institutions will find a synthesis with democratic governance at the state level. Local institutions that hold age and sex based hierarchies out of tradition especially will find difficulty in such a merger. In this light, Sudan is a candidate for a non-democratic polity that suffers a serious governance deficit.

Obviously, deficient governance at the national level also hampers the efforts of local governance to operate in the bid to promote peace and democracy.

History has shown that a governance deficit often looms large in totalitarian states and under dictatorial regimes. In such countries, Sudan included, local governance efforts are often subverted by national policy designs predicated on stifling peoples' initiatives and derailing genuine local efforts to make peace happen.

With these points in mind, the following section of the paper elaborates on governance deficit conditions in an attempt to explain the likelihood that, in Africa, as in many other similar circumstances, these could be exploited by those who harbour the ill will to commit crimes against humanity.

African Democratic Governance Deficit

The majority of African countries live under democratically elected governments, with better governance records than during the 1980s and early 1990s, when over two-thirds of the continent was under one-party rule, military socialism and civil dictatorships of different persuasions. However, this seemingly laudable achievement should not direct our attention away from the fact that democracy can also be used as an instrument of subjugation, particularly in countries ruled by majoritarian tyranny or civil authoritarianism. Although it is arguable that political crises and turmoils are the testing ground for the ability of any democracy to survive the wrath of power-hungry politicians, their capacity to exploit political frictions over severe ethnic, regional, economic and social divisions gives them a precarious start.

In assessing African democracies, three major governance deficits have persisted:

The ethnic nature of political institutions, where ethnic or racial mobilization has historically been an accomplice to genocide. Second, the prominence of patron-client relationships, which have lately developed into militarised systems of elaborate networks of warlords. Third, the absence of internal institutional and party democracy fosters minority exclusion and conflates nation or ethnicity and state.

1. Ethnic nature of political institutions

Although not all ethnically based political institutions lean to committing genocide and ethnocide, they do have the potential to be used as such if the ethos of democratic governances is not sufficiently consolidated. Ethnic mobilization is so prominent in the case of the Rwanda genocide, the wars in Liberia, Sierra Leone, Ivory Coast and the Sudan, that its association with governance deficit offers a fertile ground for ethnically motivated ethnocide or genocide. This is particularly so when the prevailing political, social and economic conditions lend themselves to the use of brute force to solve such complex problems.

2. Patron-client relationships

Because patronage traditionally benefited the chiefs, strengthening the stronghold of ethnicity in alliance with the political elite of their ethnic group, it is understandable that those left out of the political spoils consider violence or corruption as the only means available for a more just share of power.

Under conditions of poverty, meagre job opportunities and shrinking environmental space, patronage relations can be transformed into modern private armies controlled by warlords, who use desperate youth as the backbone of their troops. The civil wars in Liberia, Sierra Leone, Somalia, and Democratic Republic of Congo have all produced a large following of youth and child soldiers who have committed some of the most horrifying crimes against humanity. Also, it is difficult not to correlate the presence of a patron-client relationship with severe democratic deficit, whereby the institutions of democracy are hijacked by the few powerful and wealthy, merely to increase their wealth and power.

3. Minority exclusion and the conflation of state and nation

The violent repercussions of these politically motivated acts of exclusion are well known. Exclusion goes further than targeting specific ethnicities to stifle competitive politics, which is achieved by excluding political opponents based on their 'racial impurity' or by withdrawing their citizenship. The latter inflicted on to ex-President Kaunda of Zambia, who, after his citizenship was taken, was renounced and whose supporters were suppressed, imprisoned and killed. Similarly, the exclusion of the former Prime Minister of Cote d'Ivoire, Alassane Dramane Ouattara, from presidential elections in 1996 and 2000, respectively, by claiming that he is not an Ivorian, culminated in the current mayhem in that country.[3] Georges (2004) states that more detrimental to democratization than the reluctance of incumbents to leave office is the political manipulation of exclusionary notions of citizenship, which is reinforced by competition over scarce resources and socioeconomic opportunities in crisis situations.[4]

First, ethnicity, one of the major pillars of African political organizing, has been abused by the elite for using it as an institutional framework for mobilizing unruly and at times violent vigilantes groups during election times. In other circumstances, ethnic groups have been mobilized to commit crimes against humanity, including genocide against those who the dominant political elite perceived as their political enemies (Rwanda, Darfur, Liberia, Sierra Leone, Democratic Republic of Congo, Northern Uganda, Ethiopia, Eritrea, Ivory Coast and Northern Nigeria, only to mention the prominent cases). If not genocide, the mobilization of ethnic groups can also lead to ethnocide and ethnic cleansing, features common to local conflicts in Africa, which are often solved by local governance institutions even before they become news' headlines.

Second, the traditional African patron-client relationship and the chiefly institutions behind it have been greatly distorted by long colonization and the creeping in of new legislative and modern laws that have simultaneously eroded traditional conflict management systems. Although such systems are still very effective in dealing with localized conflicts, the state monopoly over inter-state institutions, state imposed laws, personnel and administrative control measures means that traditional African institutions are under duress. In these circumstances and under the situation of abject poverty, the patron-client relationship has in some cases been transformed into modern warlords' institutions capable of manipulating ethnic sentiments, as well as cheap armies of unemployed youth.

Third, without exception, the countries where democracy has failed are the very ones that ushered in the severest in the magnitude of crimes against humanity. To this extent, it is possible to delineate the linkages between democratic deficits at the level of political organization, abuse of ethnicity, the distortion and inhibitions imposed by the state on local governance institutions and the incidence of crimes against humanity in the case studies mentioned above. The following section of the paper uses Darfur as a case in context in order to illustrate these points.

Governance Deficit & Genocide in Darfur

Despite the difference in time, space, religion, ethnicity, culture and level of development, the main unifying factor of all acts of genocide is that they were committed by fascist, Nazi, authoritarian, autocratic and/or highly militarized regimes. Horrifyingly, they all adhere to the same pattern graphically described by *The Genocide Convention*, adopted by the United Nations in 1948, which includes the following crimes committed with the intent to destroy a national, ethnic, racial or religious group:

1. Killing members of the group;
2. Causing serious bodily or mental harm to members of the group;
3. Forcibly transferring children of the group to another group;
4. Deliberately inflicting on the group conditions of life calculated to bring about its physical destruction;
5. Imposing measures intended to prevent births within the group.

The authoritarian nature and the democratic deficit of the Sudanese regime are illustrated by the fact that it came to power in 1989 through a military coup. It advocated militant Islam and invoked Jihad in the war in South Sudan and other areas that resisted its rule. However, when the military wing of the government lead by President Al Bashir realised that Al-Turabi, then Speaker of Parliament, manipulated the governing National Congress Party, to bolster his position and undermine that of his political opponents, Al-Ba-shir introduced a state of emergency on December 12 1999. He dissolved the National Assembly in order to end what he called 'the duality of decision-making in government'. Al-Bashir claimed that Al-Turabi had begun to inter-fere in the appointment of the Federal States' Governors (including Darfur, the stronghold of the NIF support) in order to influence the forthcoming presiden-tial elections. In February 2000, Al-Turabi was officially banned from addres-sing public meeting and rallies for fear that he would incite some of his devout followers to mobilise and generate social unrest and disturbances against the "peace process".

The establishment of the Popular Defence Forces (PDFs) followed a practice initiated by the government of Sadig Al-Mahdi (1986-1989), who in 1986 established militia to counteract the National Islamic Front (NIF) militia and to serve in the war against the Sudan People's Liberation Army (SPLA). These militias were responsible for atrocities committed against communities in southern Sudan.[5]

The creation of PDFs has drastically changed the composition of the Sudanese military establishment. By 1996, the PDF vastly outnumbered the regular army, whose officer ranks were drastically depleted by repeated elimination. PDFs constitute more than 50 per cent of the Sudanese armed forces.

Principally, tribal militias such as the Janjaweed are part of the PDFs; a para-military force established by the Sudan Government, which is intended to act on behalf of the state when the Sudan Armed Forces or other security organs are unable to fulfil their function as part of the machinery of government. In a sense, through creating the PDFs, the Sudanese state handed over the mono-poly over the use of force and coercion to a parallel paramilitary security or-gan that has officially become part of the machinery of government. In these circumstances, the distinction between the Sudan Armed Forces and the Janja-weed is superfluous. Therefore, Janjaweed could be defined as "a generic term to describe Arab militia acting, under the authority, with the support, compli-city or tolerance of the Sudanese State authorities, and who benefit from im-punity for their actions".[6]

However, although the essence of the definition is correct, the use of Arab militia simplifies the complex ethnic composition of the population of Darfur in terms of Arabs and Africans. Some of the Janjaweed belong to ethnic groups that are originally African but through acculturation have acquired an Arab identity or the Arab language. It is erroneous to reduce the Janjaweed zeal to fight on behalf of the NIF government on pure racial or religious grounds. It is also erroneous to claim that there is a war of all-against-all based on racial grounds among Darfur ethic groups claiming an Arab ancestry or African Muslim ethnic identity.

Therefore, the emergence of the three main Darfur liberation movements – the Sudan Liberation Movement/Sudan Liberation Army (SLM/SLA), the Justice and Equality Movement (JEM)and the National Movement for Reform and Development (NMRD) - and their struggle against the oppressive government of the Sudan could be explained against the backdrop of marginalization and suppression of Darfurian aspirations for autonomy and development. The fact that they waged their armed struggle soon after the split of the NIF is not accidental. The NIF use of brute force and mobilization of the Janjaweed militia is also part of the pattern established since its ascendance to power in 1989 in South Sudan, the Nuba Mountains and the Southern Blue Nile, where tribal militia have ravaged the lives of thousands of innocent civilians.

Examining the grievances of the Darfurian liberation movements against the backdrop of the governance deficit of the Sudanese government would direct our attention to at least five characteristics common to all cases of genocide or ethnocide in history. These are as follows:

1. In common with other cases of ethnocide and genocide, the Sudan suffers severe governance deficit whereby a highly militarized regime uses paramilitary forces (the Janjaweed) that belong to a distinctive ethnic group (Arabized nomadic and semi-nomadic groups called Baggara or cattle owning people) to commit horrific human rights atrocities against their political opponents. These opponents are subjected to systematic killing, brutal displacement, burning of property and looting of live-

stock in order to break their will to fight for their cultural, social, political and economic rights.

2. Ethnocide and genocide in Darfur is mostly directly sponsored by a non-democratic government, which came to power through a military coup, and is supported by extremist religious forces that do not subscribe to the ethos of democratic governance outlined in the introduction of this paper. In governments where the governors are not responsive to the legitimate demands of the governed, legitimacy is often drawn from the use of power and coercion rather than through authority or the legitimate use of state power.

3. In the Sudan case, although the victims of genocide share some of the religious characteristics of those who commit genocide (Islam), the victims belong to distinct ethnic groups who claim an African ancestry. They also form communities with a shared language who consider themselves both by history and ethnic belonging indigenous to Darfur.

4. Displacement of large populations from the region of fertile to desert conditions resembles acts of deportation committed in all known genocides (e.g. the deportation of the Armenians, the Jews, the Kurds in Iraq). Land conflicts, which were traditionally solved between and among communities, have developed into acts of ethnic cleansing and depopulation of large tracts of land with the aim of starving what is perceived by the government as the heartland of the "enemy".

5. Instead of defending the victims of ethnocide, government troops have become party to the violence or have kept a blind eye to the atrocities committed by the paramilitary troops, which they have trained, armed and offered logistical support. It is a common feature of all genocides that they were committed in most cases with direct government involvement.

Conclusions

The existence of an overwhelming correlation between genocide and ethnocide and the governance deficit in Africa in general and Sudan, in particular, is disquieting. Therefore, the debate on democratic governance has much wider implications for Africa and other societies than merely the form of government. Democracy is a first step in the struggle against totalitarian forces that resort to inhumane practices to impose their whim on others, including ethnocide and genocide.

The analogies, structural parallels and similarities of the conditions of genocide in Darfur with other recent and historical cases of genocide are disquieting. The question is whether genocide should be so narrowly defined to include only those in Article II of *The Genocide Convention*. The conditions under Article II all refer to physical acts of genocide. I would like to introduce the question if we should instead include the acts mentioned in Article III under the definition of genocide. Article III has much wider connotations, including conspiracy to commit genocide, direct and public incitement to commit genocide, attempts to commit genocide and complicity in genocide.

Notes

1. World Bank (1992) defines governance as the way power is exercised in managing a country's economic resources.
2. Brinkerhoff: 2002; Minu: 2002; Olowu and Sako: 2002; Agubuzu: 2004; Mohamed Salih: 2001 and Frensch: 2004.
3. Human Rights News (New York, April 13, 2005).
4. Georges Nzongola-Ntalaja (2004), pp. 403 – 409.
5. See Mohamed Salih (1989, 1995) and Mohamed Salih and Harir (1994).
6. United Nations Report, 25 January 2005, p. 33.

References

Agubuzu, O.L.C., *African Development and Governance Strategies in the 21st Century: Looking Back to Move Forward - Essays in Honour of Adebayo Adedeji at Seventy* (London 2004).

Brinkerhoff, D. W., 'Democratic Governance and Sectoral Policy Reform: Tracin Linkages and Exploring Synergies', in: *World Develop*ment, vol. 28, no. 4 (2000) p. 601-615.

Frensch, R. 'Public Governance as Source of Quality and Variety gains from Transition', in: The Journal of Comparative Economics, 32 (2004) p. 388-408.

Georges, Nzongola-Ntalaja, 'Citizenship, Political Violence and Democratization in Africa', in: *Global Governance: A Review of Multilateralism and International Organizations*, Vol. 10, No. 4 (2004) p. 403 – 409.

Human Rights Watch, Human Rights News (New York, April 13, 2005)

Minu, Hemmati, *Multi-stakeholder Processes for Governance and Sustainability: Beyond Deadlock and Conflict* (London 2002).

Olowu, Dele, and Soumana Sako, *Better Governance and Public Policy: Capacity Building for Democratic Renewal in Africa* (Bloomfield 2003).

Salih, M.A. Mohamed, 'New Wine in Old Bottles: Tribal Militias and the Sudanese State', *in Review of African Political Economy*, No. 45/46 (1989) p. 168-74.

Salih, M.A. Mohamed, 'Ethnocide and Genocide in the Nuba Mountains', in *Geojournal: International Journal of Physical, Biological and Geography and Applications in Environmental Planning and Ecology*, Vol 36, No.1 (1995) p. 71-78.

Salih, M.A. Mohamed, African Democracies and African Politics (London 2001).

United Nations, Report of the International Commission of Inquiry on Darfur to the United Nations Secretary General, (New York: United Nations, 25 January 2005).

World Bank: *Governance and Development*. Washington, D.C. 1992 p. 58.

Nick Grono

DARFUR: THE INTERNATIONAL COMMUNITY'S FAILURE TO PROTECT

November 29th 2005

What we have seen in Darfur since early 2003 is a process of ethnic cleansing taking place before the world's eyes. What makes this all the more tragic is that policy-makers and leaders around the world are aware of what is happening there. They cannot plead ignorance. Thanks to the work of Human Rights Watch, and my organization, International Crisis Group, and others such as columnist Nick Kristof of the New York Times, these atrocities are well documented. Yet despite all the evidence, the international community has utterly failed in its responsibility to protect the people of Darfur.

There has been no shortage of forceful statements from world leaders about what is going on. On September 9th 2004, Secretary of State Colin Powell testified before Congress that "... genocide has been committed in Darfur and the government of Sudan and the Janjaweed bear responsibility". Such statements by Powell have been echoed by President George W. Bush. After visiting Darfur in October 2004, British prime minister Tony Blair declared "We can't have a situation where thousands of people are dying, and nothing is done". He also assured that the international focus would not fade while the situation continued.

The violence in Darfur has also been condemned by influential international organizations. United Nations Secretary General Kofi Annan noted towards the end of 2004 that "There are strong indications that war crimes and crimes against humanity have occurred in Darfur on a large and systematic scale..." The European Council followed suit and declared in June 2005 that "The Council continues to be deeply concerned at the serious infringements of human rights and of international humanitarian law committed against the civilian population in Darfur."

Clearly, there has been no lack of moral outrage about the horrors taking place in Darfur. Despite these firm statements international action has not lived up to the rhetoric.

International Action

So what action has the international community taken? A multitude of international actors, composed of multilateral, unilateral and non-governmental institutions, have a wide variety of tools at their disposal to actively engage in Darfur. Starting with the UN, the Security Council has a number of tools open to it to pressure governments. The UN can send fact-finding missions, it can impose sanctions and no-fly zones. Another tool available to the UN is to refer situations to the International Criminal Court. When deemed necessary, it can take more forceful action - such as peacekeeping missions or, in the most extreme circumstances, it can authorize peace enforcement missions, that is, armed intervention.

In the case of Darfur, the Security Council has been appallingly slow to put any real pressure on the Sudanese government. The Council finally took action in July 2004 (resolution 1556) with a largely meaningless arms embargo on the Janjaweed militias and the rebels. It also required Khartoum to disarm the Janjaweed or face sanctions. In March 2005 (resolution 1591), some eight months later, and in the face of repeated provocations from the Sudanese government – including its utter failure to disarm the Janjaweed – the Security Council belatedly decided to impose a broader range of sanctions, and appointed a Sanctions Committee to decide on whom sanctions should be applied to, aided by a Panel of Experts to advise the Committee.

That was eight months ago. However, the Panel of Experts has yet to make its report, so needless to say, no sanctions have been applied so far. And it is highly unlikely that there will be any sanctions before the end of this year. The Security Council has, however, taken more robust action on the legal front. In September 2004 (resolution 1564), it asked the Secretary-General to establish an international commission of inquiry to investigate violations of international human rights and humanitarian law. That Commission of Inquiry issued its report in January 2005. Its report makes for harrowing reading, documenting repeated systematic crimes against humanity and war crimes. The Commission concluded that:

> "[T]he Government of Sudan and the Janjaweed are responsible for serious violations of international human rights and humanitarian law amounting to crimes under international law. In particular, the Commission found that Government forces and militias conducted indiscriminate attacks, including killing of civilians, torture, enforced disappearances, destruction of villages, rape and other forms of sexual violence, pillaging and forced displacement, throughout Darfur."

The Commission also concluded that the Government of Sudan had not pursued a policy of genocide.

Finally, in March 2005, the Security Council referred the situation in Darfur to the International Criminal Court for investigation. The ICC opened its investigation into Darfur the following June.

The other key international actor on Darfur has been the African Union. The African Union was only established in 2002 to replace the discredited Organization of African Unity. Its Peace and Security Council became operational in early 2004. Darfur has been a test case for the fledgling organization and, although it has performed reasonably well within its limited resources and mandate, the limitations of its capabilities are being exposed.

The African Union established a small monitoring mission in Darfur in mid-2004, consisting of some 60 monitors, and 300 troops to protect them. It decided to expand the mission to 3,300 in October that same year and to 7,700 in April of the following year. However a large gap between intentions and capabilities has become apparent. The AU mission has still not fully deployed its full complement of 7,700 troops, police and observers. And those 7,700 are expected to patrol an area roughly the size of France. Another critical limitation of the AU mission is its mandate as it is largely an observer mission. Under this mission the AU does not have a mandate to proactively protect civilians. In fact, it can only protect civilians in the most restricted of circumstances. Its mandate makes this all too clear, authorizing it to:

"protect civilians whom it encounters under imminent threat and in the immediate vicinity, within resources and capacity, it being understood that the protection of the civilian population is the responsibility of the GoS [Government of Sudan]."

The other key role of the AU has been to facilitate the erratic peace talks between the Sudan government and the rebels now taking place in Abuja, Nigeria. Those talks started in September 2005 and have been through six rounds so far, with the seventh round starting November 28 – but there has been little progress to date.

That leaves the European Union, NATO and the United States as the remaining key international actors. The approach of the European Union has largely been to support the work of the African Union. The EU has made it clear that it sees the AU as the lead international player in Darfur, and that the EU's role is primarily to support African solutions to African problems. This it has done by providing financial support to the AU and its mission in Darfur – some 150 million euros to date - and limited logistical and planning support.

NATO has been a strategic competitor of the EU in Darfur. Last year, as it cast around for a way to get involved in Africa and peace operations more broadly, NATO concluded that it could play a constructive role in Darfur. The policy of NATO involves offering expertise and logistical support to the AU mission. However, that offer led to an unseemly squabble with the EU about which organization was better suited to support the AU, and resulted in them both getting involved. Yet, currently NATO has no intention of going beyond its limited support and logistical role, and the organization will not put troops on the ground in any significant numbers.

On the level of individual nations, the United States has a mixed record on Darfur. In its rhetoric the US has been at the forefront of international action, Colin Powell and George W. Bush both having called Darfur a genocide. Powell visited Darfur in 2004, and Condoleezza Rice went the following year. Her deputy, Bob Zoellick, who has the lead on Darfur for the Administration, has been to Darfur four times in 2005 alone. Also, the US has been generous in its aid contributions, supplying well over half the food supplies to the displaced Darfurians. And in perhaps their most significant move to date, the US abstained from the Security Council vote on the ICC referral, allowing the referral to go through – a very significant step for an Administration that had made opposition to the ICC a leading plank of its foreign policy till then.

Recently the Senate passed the Darfur Peace and Accountability Act, which would significantly increase pressure on Khartoum if it is passed by the House of Representatives. But then a congressional committee cut a proposed $50 million contribution to the AU from a budget bill. Despite this the US still remains one of the key players in forcing further action on Darfur, and civil society should focus on pressing the U.S. to do more.

Apart from governments and international organizations, a role is played by aid and humanitarian groups, and other NGOs. Darfur has achieved its prominence on the international stage in no small part because of the work of International Crisis Group, Human Rights Watch and Amnesty International. Around the world, and particularly in the US, there are advocacy organizations working very effectively to mobilize grass roots support for stronger international action on Darfur.

Aid agencies such as the World Food Program, and humanitarian NGOs such as Médecins Sans Frontières, CARE, Oxfam and countless others have done a magnificent job in providing aid and ensuring that the humanitarian situation in Darfur is not far worse. It is largely due to their efforts that mortality rates for over 2 million displaced persons have been significantly reduced over the last year or so. But aid and humanitarian agencies can only do so much. To a large extent the Government of Sudan is content to let them do their work. Khartoum has largely succeeded in its aim of forcing Darfurians into camps where they can be controlled and monitored, and kept alive by the international community.

The Current Situation

Until a couple of months ago, it appeared that the situation was beginning to stabilize into yet another low intensity African conflict, albeit one with over 2 million displaced persons, and more than 200,000 refugees in neighboring Chad. But recent weeks have seen renewed Janjaweed atrocities and unsubstantiated reports of government attacks on villages in Western Darfur. Rebel groups have been fighting among themselves, and aid workers have been attacked, leading some agencies to consider pulling out. The upsurge in fighting

43

is also threatening to destabilize neighboring Chad and potentially cause it to spiral into its own civil war. While this situation continues, none of the 2.5 million displaced persons and refugees can return to their destroyed villages.

We often talk in generalities when we discuss the horrors of Darfur and other conflicts. Sometimes its takes the specifics of atrocities to remind us of the human dimension of what is taking place while the world stands by. Nicholas Kristof, a columnist at the New York Times, is currently in Darfur. He has been to the region five times in the last couple of years, and his powerful first hand accounts of what is going on in Darfur have played a large role in mobilizing grassroots support in the US. In February 2005, he published a number of photos that he had obtained from the AU mission. The first shows a young boy killed by the Janjaweed. His mother was dead next to him. The second shows the corpse of a man with an injured leg who was apparently unable to run away when the Janjaweed militia attacked. The last is the skeleton of a man or woman whose wrists are still bound. The attackers pulled the person's clothes down to the knees, presumably so the victim could be sexually abused before being killed. And last week Kristof provided powerful testimony of the continuing mass violence in Darfur. In his column he said:

"Noura is one of thousands of women and girls to be gang-raped in Darfur, as part of what appears to be a deliberate Sudanese government policy to break the spirit of several African tribes through mass rape."

"Saida Abdukarim, also 25, was tending her vegetables when three men with guns seized her. She pleaded with them, pointing out that she is eight months' pregnant. They said, 'You are black, and so we can rape you,' she recalled. Then they gang-raped her and beat her with sticks and their guns..."

Responsibility to Protect

The UN held a World Summit in New York in September 2005 to celebrate the 60th anniversary of the United Nations. It was the largest-ever gathering of world leaders. There was hope that the Summit would agree on major reforms to the UN and take bold decisions on human rights, security and development.

In the end, the Summit was a disappointment, with member states largely failing to take strong action on any of these fronts. However one significant success was the agreement to acknowledge the doctrine of responsibility to protect as an international responsibility. Specifically the Summit agreed to the following:

> "Each individual State has the responsibility to protect its populations from genocide, war crimes, ethnic cleansing and crimes against humanity. This responsibility entails the prevention of such crimes, including their incitement, through appropriate and necessary means. We accept that responsibility and will act in accordance with it."

This is an historic step, because until now state sovereignty was formally, if not in practice, sacrosanct. This is perhaps understandable – no state wants to be the object of coercive intervention by others. But of course there are situations, such as Rwanda or Kosovo, that such intervention is the only way to stop genocide and other atrocities. Now, for the first time, the UN has explicitly recognized that there are circumstances in which failures by states to protect their own populations gives rise to an obligation by the international community to intervene in that state's sovereign affairs.

Such a responsibility is vested first with the sovereign state itself, but when they are unwilling or unable to ensure such protections, that responsibility must be borne by the broader community of states. The responsibility to protect (R2P in short form) is about much more than intervention. It extends to a whole continuum of obligations from the responsibility to *prevent* crises, to *react* to situations of compelling human need, and to *rebuild* in post-conflict situations, including recovery, reconstruction and reconciliation.

Applying this to Darfur, Khartoum has the primary responsibility to protect its own population. Through its active involvement in the slaughter and displacement of civilians in Darfur, it has clearly and wantonly failed in that responsibility. The issue then arises as to whether the situation is such that the international community should intervene.

There are five criteria governing the legitimacy of such intervention. The first is Just Cause. There must be a large scale loss of life or 'ethnic cleansing', whether carried out by killing, forced expulsion, acts of terror or rape. In the case of Darfur, it is clear that this test has been satisfied. The second criteria is Right Intention. If the international community did decide to coercively intervene in Darfur, through the African Union or anyone else, there is no doubt this test would be satisfied.

The third is Last Resort. In Darfur, this criterion must be very close to being satisfied. Non-military international pressure has been slowly intensifying on Sudan – not least the Security Council resolutions on sanctions and the ICC referral. However, there is more pressure that can be applied if the political will is there – starting with the robust implementation of those sanctions and the targeting of Sudan's oil industry. And perhaps the last step remaining to be taken before this criteria is fulfilled is to push for a significant expansion of the AU force – doubling it to 12-15,000 troops and giving it a much stronger civilian protection mandate. In the event that the AU is unable or unwilling to take this step, Crisis Group argues that NATO should provide a bridging force.

The fourth of the five criteria is Proportional Means. This is where it gets difficult. One has to assume, on its past behavior and all its public statements, that the Government of Sudan will not agree to an international intervention force. It is prepared to tolerate the small African Union force, with its limited mandate – but probably not much more. The preferable option is that adopted for East Timor – getting Sudan's consent, however reluctant, to a large external civilian protection force of 12-15,000 strong. This would clearly be proportional to the objective. Armed intervention on the other hand would require a much larger force. In such a non-permissive environment, General Roméo Dallaire, the UN commander in Rwanda during the genocide, estimates that a force of some 44,000 troops would be required to achieve the objectives of such intervention.

The final criteria is Reasonable Prospects. If Sudan agreed to an expanded civilian protection force with a stronger mandate, then the prospects would be good for such a force to achieve its objectives. However, if Sudan does not agree to such a force, then the situation and prospects will be far less attractive. In such a non-permissive situation, the international community would be sending in an armed force into a region the size of France. It would be at risk of attack not only from the Janjaweed militias, but also from government troops. Government forces number some 100,000, and the Janjaweed another few thousand more. Since Iraq, we are all much more aware of the potentially disastrous consequences of armed intervention in a hostile environment. It is pretty clear that the international community does not have the stomach to provide this kind of force right now, particularly in light of the Iraq experience – and it is doubtful if it ever will. Government of Sudan's actions are constantly being calibrated against the willingness of the international community to take more robust action, with the ultimate objective of ensuring that the international community has no cause to push for this final step.

What needs to be done now

Notwithstanding the obligations of Sudan as outlined above, and those of the international community in the face of continued intransigence of Sudan, there is more that can be done outside of armed intervention. Crisis Group has repeatedly argued that the international community needs to pursue three objectives in Darfur.

The first is that of civilian protection. This African Union Peace and Security Council must give its mission in Darfur a mandate that focuses unequivocally on the protection of civilians. The mission must be authorized to use all necessary measures against threats to civilians and humanitarian operations. The force on ground must be significantly expanded from 7,700 to 12-15,000 personnel. This is the minimum to enable the mission to fulfill its expanded mandate – namely protecting civilians, enabling the return of displaced persons and refugees, and ensuring that Khartoum lives up to its repeated promises to reign in the Janjaweed. Ideally the expanded force should be provided by the African Union and within the next 60 days. If the AU cannot meet these objectives – numbers and quality of troops, and time – NATO should work closely with the AU to deploy its own bridging force and bring the total force up to 12,000 to 15,000 and maintain it at that level until the AU can perform the mission entirely with its own personnel.

The second objective is to implement accountability in Darfur. This means putting in place the UN sanctions straight away and widening the sanctions to target Sudan's oil industry. And it means supporting the ICC investigation – the AU and member states should provide relevant information on a timely basis to the ICC. Member states should also make sure that the ICC has the resources needed to thoroughly investigate Darfur.

47

The third objective is to build a Darfur peace process. This implies that the Government of Sudan delegation must represent the new Government of National Unity – meaning it must include representatives of the southern SPLM, and not just the hard-line National Congress Party. The international community – the US, UK, France, Norway, EU, Canada and the UN – must agree on a common position for the direction of the negotiations. And more support needs to be provided to the two main rebel movements, the SLA and JEM, to unify their negotiating positions. The peace process must remain a focus, as in the end the solution to the conflict in Darfur will be found in a negotiated settlement.

Following that overview of international engagement in Darfur, the key message remains that there is much more that the international community can do to stop the atrocities occurring on a daily basis in Darfur. But more than two years into the conflict we are beginning to see a decrease in moral outrage over Darfur and international community fatigue. The fear is that we will soon settle for Darfur as a low intensity conflict, handing over responsibility to the humanitarian agencies – as we have in so many other places in Africa – only to look back in a decade or so and vow "never again", when it was within our means to ensure that it never happened on this scale in the first place.

Mr. Juan E. Méndez

POSSIBILITIES FOR GENOCIDE PREVENTION

13 December 2005

The situation in Darfur and the suffering experienced by its so-called "African tribes" has been of grave concern to me since I was appointed Special Adviser to the Secretary-General on the Prevention of Genocide in July 2004. Shortly after taking on my functions, in September 2004, I visited Darfur at the Secretary-General's request together with the High Commissioner for Human Rights. I visited Sudan again in September of this year to review the situation from the perspective of the prevention of genocide and to observe the changes that took place since my last visit. My intention was to analyze the relative effectiveness of the measures the High Commissioner and I had proposed in October 2004 during our briefing to the Security Council.

Although many of you might be aware of my mandate and its background, I would like to provide you with an overview and share some general thoughts on the prevention of genocide that should be relevant for the understanding of the particular challenges that the situation in Darfur presents for the International Community as a whole and for my office in particular.

The Mandate of the Special Adviser to the Secretary-General on the Prevention of Genocide

The source of my mandate is Security Council Resolution 1366 (2001), which the Council approved in an effort to acknowledge the lessons learned from the failure to prevent such tragedies as the genocide in Rwanda and the massacre in Srebrenica. Important guidance on the interpretation of this mandate derives from its background and history. On the one hand, the creation of the position of Special Adviser on the Prevention of Genocide is part of an Action Plan presented by the Secretary-General on the 10th anniversary of the Rwanda Genocide to the Commission on Human Rights, on 7 April 2004. On the other hand, the mandate has to be seen in the wider context of UN efforts to create a culture of prevention and the previous discussions regarding the prevention of massive violations of human rights and humanitarian law.

The independent International Commission on Intervention and State Sovereignty, which was established by Canada to look in the question of whether and when the international community should intervene to protect civilian populations, strongly believed that the so-called responsibility to protect implies an accompanying responsibility to prevent. The Commission established that, with regard to massive violations, what is lacking is not so much the basic data, but its analysis and translation into policy prescriptions, as well as the will to do something about it. The Secretary-General's High-level Panel on Threats, Challenges and Change endorsed the notion that there is a collective international responsibility to protect, to be exercised by the Security Council and which should include the authorization of military intervention as a last resort, in the event of genocide and other large-scale killing, ethnic cleansing or serious violations of international humanitarian law. The Panel also recommended referring cases to the International Criminal Court at an early stage to deter parties to a conflict from committing crimes against humanity, war crimes or genocide.

Since world leaders came together at United Nations Headquarters in New York for the World-Summit commemorating the Organization's 60th anniversary, many commentators expressed their disappointment that the meeting did not produce a consensus for the deep reforms that the United Nations needs. However, from the point of view of my mandate, the assessment of the Outcome Document is much more favorable. First, I am encouraged by the full support for my work expressed by Member States in the document. Second, the responsibility to protect populations from genocide, war crimes, ethnic cleansing and crimes against humanity, enshrined in the document, establishes a moral principle in international affairs that was long overdue after the experience of collective international failure in cases such as Rwanda and Srebrenica.

My office cannot be regarded at present as a universal early-warning and early-action mechanism for the prevention of genocide worldwide, but rather an effort to improve the United Nations' response to situations of potential massive violations of human rights and humanitarian law that have an ethnic, racial, religious or national character. This is an effort that requires strong support from Member States, NGOs, academia and others.

The purpose of the Special Adviser is not to determine whether genocide has occurred or is occurring, but to propose steps to prevent it. I am approaching my mandate pragmatically. The last paragraph of the outline of my mandate states clearly that *"the Special Adviser would not make a determination on whether genocide within the meaning of the Convention had occurred."* I prefer to see this limitation not as a reflection of political sensitivities, but as a practical one deriving from the preventive character of my mandate. My role is to provide early warning before all the elements are present that constitute the definition of genocide under the Convention of 1948 and to suggest appropriate action. Too often the debate over whether genocide is occurring has become more important than taking action to reverse the situation and prevent further violations.

The mandate of the Special Adviser on the Prevention of Genocide involves gathering information, providing early warning and presenting appropriate recommendations to prevent a situation from degenerating into genocide. The functions of the Adviser were outlined to the Council as follows: (1) Collecting existing information, in particular from within the UN system, on massive and serious violations of human rights and international humanitarian law of ethnic and racial origin that, if not prevented or halted, might lead to genocide; (2) Acting as an early-warning mechanism to the Secretary-General, and, through him to the Security Council, by bringing to the latter's attention potential situations that could result in genocide; (3) Making recommendations to the Security Council through the Secretary-General, on actions to prevent or halt genocide; and (4) Liaising with the UN system on activities for the prevention of genocide and working to enhance the UN capacity to analyze and manage information relating to genocide and related crimes.

Beyond the current debate on the responsibility to protect, preventing genocide is already a legal obligation deriving from the 1948 Convention and its application as *jus cogens*. Thus, preventing genocide is a principle of international law so fundamental that no nation may ignore it.

Early warning and early action to prevent genocide

Given its limited resources, my office acts as a focal point for early-warning information coming from sources inside and outside the UN system. According to my mandate to advise the Secretary-General and the Security Council of situations of massive violations, I take up country situations presented to me on a case-by-case basis. In doing so, the starting point is the legal definition of the crime of genocide and other punishable acts according to the Convention of 1948. Accordingly, information needs to point towards the existence of a national, ethnic, racial or religious group at risk.

Both in the short and long term, the prevention of genocide seems predicated on acting comprehensively in four interrelated areas: the protection of populations at risk against serious or massive violations of human rights or humanitarian law; establishing accountability for violations of human rights and humanitarian law; humanitarian relief and access to basic economic, social and cultural rights; and steps to address underlying causes of conflict through peace agreements and transitional processes.

The protection of populations at risk will sometimes require deployment of international forces, both military and police forces. Occasionally the only way to prevent a humanitarian catastrophe will be to order such deployment regardless of the consent of the local authorities. We must be ready to take that ultimate step, but we must also act with a sense of responsibility not to make matters worse; recent examples of non-consensual use of force do not give us any sense of comfort that such actions will always help and never hurt the innocent. For the most part, however, it is possible to deploy international protective forces with the consent of the government involved, and, if that possibility is available, it will always be preferable.

Accountability in the form of punishment for genocide, crimes against humanity and war crimes is crucial to prevention of similar acts in the future. The sense of impunity for the crimes already committed breeds insecurity among the populations at risk and creates an incentive for repetition among the perpetrators. Breaking the cycle of impunity is greatly aided by the existence of an institution like the permanent International Criminal Court (ICC). However, we must realize that it will be important to press the domestic judicial authorities to assume their responsibilities, and for civil society to contribute efforts towards a comprehensive set of policy prescriptions that will meet everybody's expectations of justice and to do so with respect for international standards of fair trial and due process.

Humanitarian relief and access to basic economic, social and cultural rights is important to prevent loss of life from continuing after the initial killings have ceased, and also to avoid placing populations at risk under conditions of life designed to bring about their extinction. In addition, by their very presence, international civilian monitors and relief workers can provide a basic measure of protection to the population they serve.

Finally, it is important to pursue the resolution of conflicts that can deteriorate into genocide. Peace will be the ultimate prevention of genocide, but, in order to have that effect, it must be a lasting peace, one that tries to avoid winners and losers and that is more than a mere cessation of hostilities. Most important, it must be a peace that addresses the danger of spoilers in the peace process, while not rewarding them with impunity. The resolution must address open wounds in societies that could erupt in future conflict down the road. In other words, what we must strive for is peace with justice.

The situation in Darfur

Since my appointment as Special Adviser, the situation in Darfur has been a primary concern for me. As I mentioned earlier, the first step I took upon my appointment was to visit Darfur together with the High Commissioner for Human Rights. Upon our return, in September 2004, Ms. Arbour and I briefed the Security Council on our visit and provided recommendations to enhance the protection of civilians and prevent future violations of human rights and humanitarian law.

We underscored the importance of ensuring accountability and of affording increased protection to civilians in the Internally Displaced People (IDP) camps and villages throughout Darfur. We recommended, most importantly, the deployment of a sizeable international police presence. Since then, the African Union has incorporated a civilian police component in to its Mission in Darfur.

Throughout the last year, I have expressed my concern that the reaction to the situation in Darfur was too slow and hesitant. I agree with the words of the Secretary-General, who, in requesting greater assistance for the deployment of a larger number of African Union (AU) forces, wondered whether the international community *"might have learnt nothing from Rwanda"*.

Prior to my visit in September of this year, and drawing on information from a number of reports, I was prepared to find a situation that had become much more stable. Instead, I encountered a reality that continues to be of great concern. I must underscore that I perceived an alarming gap between the authorities' view of the situation and its measures to address the problems of Darfur, and the accounts of many Darfuris and observers with whom we met during the course of the visit.

Undoubtedly there have been some positive developments over the last year. Clashes among the parties decreased during much of 2005, prior to its resurgence in September. The widespread destruction of villages of "African tribes" by Arab militia or Government forces had practically ceased and, although there are killings of civilians in the course of attacks, their number is undoubtedly smaller than at the peak of the conflict. However, the confirmed number of civilian deaths due to violence increased again from 70 in October to 120 in November.

The AU is recognized as a key factor in bringing a measure of protection to the population of the region. They are now present in larger numbers and throughout a larger portion of the territory of Darfur. Those with whom we spoke confirmed that African Mission in Sudan (AMIS) contingents provide a level of protection where they are present. AMIS is making an effort to locate civilian police in or near the larger IDP camps and has established joint patrols with the Sudanese police, including accompanying IDP women during firewood collection.

The presence of humanitarian workers has been key in avoiding major loss of life. Not only has it led to an improvement in assistance for IDPs and other vulnerable groups (in terms of food, education and health) but it has also contributed in some measure to a sense of security. However, for the past few months, secure humanitarian access to the affected populations has been extremely difficult, falling to a low of 70 per cent, the worst access levels since April 2004. The enlarged presence of the UN through the deployment of United Nations Mission in Sudan (UNMIS) personnel (particularly Human Rights

Officers and Civil Affairs Officers) is also helping better to monitor and address some of the situation in the region.

There are, however, elements of major concern that must be addressed urgently.

(1)   Protection of civilians

Notwithstanding the generally improved security trend over 2005 that I described earlier, civilians continue to be killed and some wholesale displacement of populations and burning of villages continues and have taken place during and after my visit. Many of those we spoke to were concerned that there are few villages of "African tribes" remaining to be destroyed (given that almost two million persons are living in IDP camps). The situation today is one of escalating banditry and attacks that denotes a dangerous slippage. Many of those we spoke to were worried about a possible resumption of violence in the region, particularly in North and South Darfur. There has been an increase in rebel activity and attacks by Janjaweed Arab militias, including on IDP camps and some villages. On 1 October 2005, the African Union's Special Representative in Sudan described a *"collapse of the security situation"*. Clashes between armed groups should cease immediately and must not lead to a downward spiral of violence.

I am concerned that these worrisome developments indicate a potential for greater instability as nomadic Arab tribes transit through Darfur along traditional camel and cattle routes in the months of October to December. The increased violence may be the result of posturing before and during the talks in Abuja; of action by groups with no direct representation at the talks; of unresolved tensions between ethnic communities over land tenure and use; or of some other reason. Irrespective of the origin, these episodes constitute warning signs of the precarious security conditions and of the possibility of renewed generalized violence in the region. Even without them, continuation of the status quo achieved in the last few months would be unacceptable as it imposes severe damage on Darfur's society, rendering improvement in intercommunal relations increasingly difficult. The renewed fighting in North and South Darfur and the lawlessness in West Darfur are not only reminders of that precariousness; they should also be considered dangerous signs of slippage in security.

IDPs in all camps visited reported ongoing attacks by *Janjaweed* causing a deep sense of insecurity. Women continue to be subject to sexual violence, and the property of IDPs is repeatedly looted. The situation appears to have deteriorated in that the attacks are reported to occur in the immediate vicinity, sometimes only minutes away from camps and villages, or even inside camps and villages during daylight hours. Insecurity, particularly along the perimeter of camps and villages, is of particular concern, with little discernible effort to correct the situation on the part of the authorities. The Government must be urged to consider rape under procedures that reflect the gravity of the crime and afford victims and witnesses guarantees against re-victimization. The Government of Sudan, in cooperation with UNMIS and AMIS, should promptly set up a comprehensive plan for the full implementation of its obligation to disarm the Janjaweed, including all irregular paramilitary groups and individuals who may have been introduced into the Popular Defence Forces, Border Intelligence Guard, Popular Police or Nomadic police. In addition, the Government of Sudan must indicate to the African Union Ceasefire Commission, within a deadline defined by the Security Council, those militias it controls or are under its influence, for the purpose of monitoring breaches of the ceasefire and separating criminals and bandits.

Because of distrust in the police, incidents of violations of human rights and humanitarian law involving IDPs appear to be systematically underreported. At the same time, IDPs sense that the interest and attention of the International Community seems to be decreasing. Victims remarked that criminal acts of Government of Sudan officials, even when reported, are not investigated and followed up. Victims often feel exploited by national and international interlocutors for political reasons. Many IDPs experience discrimination and derogatory language by Government of Sudan officials when trying to report incidents. Some interlocutors reported that some IDPs are beginning to take measures of self-protection.

Many IDPs are heavily traumatized and, at the same time, politicized by the parties to the conflict. In the course of their displacement, many experienced killings, rapes and looting. In addition, the difficult situation in camps has negative psychological effects on the IDPs, who in many cases already had arrived at the camps two years ago. The displacement has caused a situation of dependency on food and other day-to-day support. Life in the camps depends mainly on buying and selling basic items for survival, a behavior that many IDPs are not used to. IDPs expressed a great level of frustration over their situation.

There have been reports on the use of air support by military helicopters in recent Janjaweed attacks in Darfur. In this respect, the Security Council should demand that the Government of the Sudan immediately cease any such flights and take measures against individuals responsible for offensive military over flights as foreseen in resolution 1591.

AMIS must be commended for providing a measure of protection for civilians in Darfur. However, there is a widely felt need in the region for a reinforced mission in terms of communications, logistics and numbers. In addition, there is a sense that the mandate of AMIS could be made more robust with regard to the protection of civilians. At its present level of deployment, AMIS does not have the strength necessary to provide security for IDPs and villagers in the most vulnerable areas of the region. In addition, AMIS seem to face challenges in terms of "cash flow" for its operations (they are having problems paying their bills), logistics, and the deployment of crucial materiel that would make its presence more effective, in particular APCs for patrols.

In this regard it would be important for the Security Council to urge member states to provide AMIS with the necessary communications, logistics and transport equipment, as well as financial means, to respond promptly and effectively to the protection needs of the civilian population, in accordance with its mandate. In particular, the Security Council should demand that the Government of Sudan cooperate fully with AMIS and facilitate the deployment of AMIS assets.

Since my visit in September, a number of reports have underscored the difficulties that AMIS faces. A new Assessment Mission is underway at this very moment to evaluate the performance of AMIS and to offer recommendations to address the needs of Darfur. I trust that it will lead to more effective measures to ensure greater protection of the civilian population.

(2)   Humanitarian assistance

Though overall humanitarian access has improved visibly since my last visit, looting of humanitarian aid has led to the interruption of aid delivery to a number of areas. Although the authorities in the region claim to be taking steps to address these problems, there is a general fear that the situation could deteriorate.

The social and economic situation in camps and villages appear to have deteriorated. Some IDPs complained about the lack of registration by WFP and the lack of access to food. Often, only the solidarity of IDPs provides all affected persons with the minimum support. In the Ardamata camp in West Darfur, IDPs complained about the lack of access to education for their children and alleged that the Government of Sudan was systematically preventing children of African descent from attending school. Alcoholism and prostitution, which were unknown to many villages, are reported from many camps and are contributing to conflict and violence. The role of men in the social structure of families and tribes has changed, as they are confined to stay in the camps and are prevented from protecting the women from sexual violence. The high number and frequency of assaults on women and girls has caused deep depression and a sentiment of helplessness and insecurity among IDPs. Sometimes, around camps, IDPs enter private property to collect firewood, causing conflict with landowners. Often, IDP leaders are arrested for political reasons and subject to torture or ill treatment. Agencies from West Darfur reported that IDPs are sometimes blocked by armed Arab elements from accessing food and water around camps.

Returns are affected negatively by the overall climate of insecurity. IDPs expressed a strong desire to return to their villages provided that the Janjaweed were disarmed. Current returns seem to be limited to the planting season, and those who have returned to plant intend to return to IDP camps soon. The population deeply distrusts the police in the villages. Furthermore, almost all IDPs claimed that their land was currently occupied by members of Arab tribes. Therefore, there will also be a need to settle disputes over title and usage of lands that have been occupied after the displacement.

Much of the agricultural land of Darfur is not being cultivated, disrupting the traditional economy and lifestyle of the region. Together with displacement, and the dislocation it creates, the entire social structure of the region is affected. There is concern that tensions among communities could increase in the months of October and November, as crops become ready to harvest and as cattle herders transit throughout the region along trading routes. The Government of the Sudan, the Sudan Liberation Army (SLA) and the Justice and Equality Movement (JEM), in cooperation with AMIS and UNMIS, could identify traditional migration and grazing routes for nomads to permit the safe passage to markets in Libya and Chad. Confidence-building measures, such as the establishment of "days of peace" to allow the harvesting of crops, could also be considered.

While the delivery of humanitarian aid has provided life-saving assistance, it may also be contributing at the same time to expectations among the IDP population with regard to basic services that they never had access to in their original communities. This will have an impact upon the conditions of eventual return.

(3)   Accountability for violations

Although we received assurances from the authorities that they soon would take important steps with regard to accountability, there is a strong sense in Darfur that impunity continues to prevail. This situation has fed a deep sense of mistrust by IDPs and vulnerable groups in the justice system. We also were disappointed to learn that the cases that have been considered by the Special Court for Crimes Committed in Darfur did not deal with the major crimes committed during the conflict and involve, for the most part, cases that could have been tried in the ordinary justice system.

The Government of Sudan argued that the local courts have sufficient capacity and independence and that the referral by the Security Council interfered with the sovereignty of Sudan. However, the Security Council's referral to the ICC seems to have contributed to suppress the activities of some individuals for fear of being prosecuted. In this regard, it is important to recall the Government's obligation to cooperate fully with the Prosecutor of the International Criminal Court, as demanded in Security Council Resolution 1593. It is in the self-interest of the Government to cooperate with the ICC prosecutions as a way of creating an atmosphere conducive to reconciliation. Under

the principle of complementarity, the ICC will concentrate only on the perpetrators bearing the highest responsibility for war crimes and crimes against
humanity, thereby supporting and not interfering with efforts of the Sudanese
judiciary to bring justice to those crimes under domestic jurisdiction.

(4)   Steps towards sustainable peace

It is important to create the conditions of security that will allow for a safe
and voluntary return. A political solution reached in the Abuja talks is a priority to help bring peace to the region. At the same time, there is a strong sense
in Darfur that an inclusive, credible and grass roots process of inter-communal dialogue is needed to re-establish peaceful inter-communal relations and
re-weave the social fabric of the region. Specific measures to address property
and land usage rights will be indispensable to achieve peace and restore relations between nomadic herders and sedentary agriculturalist tribes. UNMIS
and AMIS could help facilitate credible inter-communal conferences on reconciliation at the local level.

As I have mentioned, the position of Special Adviser inscribes itself in the
broader context of the international community's efforts to prevent massive
violations of human rights and protect civilian populations. The international
community, however, faces a serious challenge to ensure that its aspirations
and the emerging norm of a responsibility to protect are translated into effective measures that help protect civilians. The situation in Darfur is, in a sense,
a litmus test to help gauge the effectiveness of our response. I trust we will be
up to the challenge.

Printed in the United States
144380LV00004B/5/A